T

With Scriptural Reflections and Prayers

Edited by
Rev. Victor Hoagland, C.P.

Illustrated by
William Luberoff

The Regina Press
New York

Nihil Obstat: Rev. Francis J. Schneider, J.C.D.
Censor Librorum
June 8, 1994

Imprimatur: Most Reverend
John R. McGann, D.D.
Bishop of Rockville Centre
June 9, 1994

The Rosary: Where Did It Come From?

Praying the rosary well is more important than knowing its history, yet knowing the origins of the rosary can teach us much about this great prayer.

The beginnings of the rosary are found in the early Christian practice of reciting the 150 psalms from the bible, either daily or weekly, as a way of prayer. Those unable to recite the psalms began to recite 150 prayers, mainly the Our Father, 150 times, often using beads to count the prayers. By medieval times the custom of saying "Paternoster" beads (the latin for Our Father) was common in many countries of Europe. While saying the prayers it was customary to meditate on the mysteries of the life of Jesus, from his birth to his resurrection.

In the rosary today, the Our Father is still said before each decade of Hail Marys and meditation on the mysteries of Jesus' life and resurrection remains at the heart of the prayer.

The rosary in its present form arose in late medieval Christianity.

The Hail Mary

The Hail Mary evolved as a prayer from the devotion of medieval men and women who saw Mary, the mother to Jesus, as the great witness to His life, death and resurrection. Its earliest form was the greeting made to Mary by the Angel Gabriel:

Hail Mary,
full of grace,
the Lord is with you   LUKE 1:28

Over time the greeting given to Mary by her cousin Elizabeth was added:

Blessed are you among women
and blessed is the fruit of your womb.

                                          LUKE 1:42

Finally by the 15th century, the remainder of the prayer appeared:

Holy Mary, mother of God,
pray for us sinners
now and at the hour of our death.

The prayer calls upon Mary, full of grace and close to her Son, to intercede for us sinners now and at the time our death. We share her as a mother with St. John to whom Jesus entrusted her, when on

4

Calvary He said, "Behold your mother." She will always bring Christ into our life. We trust her to care for us as she cared for the newly married couple at Cana in Galilee. We can go to her in our need.

By the end of the 16th century the practice of saying 150 Hail Marys in series or decades of 10 was popular among many ordinary Christian people. The mysteries of the life, death and resurrection of Jesus, contained in the Joyful, Sorrowful and Glorious Mysteries, were remembered during these prayers.

Other Prayers of the Rosary

Other traditional Christian prayers became part of the rosary such as the Apostles' Creed, an ancient summary of Christian belief. Said in the beginning of the rosary, it recalls the great truths of faith to us. The Glory Be to the Father, recited at the end of each decade, is an ancient prayer praising the Trinity of Father, Son, and Holy Spirit. Finally, the prayer, Hail, Holy Queen came to be recited at the end of the rosary.

Rosa Mystica

The name "rosary" comes from the flower, the rose, which in medieval times was seen as a symbol of life eternal. Mary, the first to be redeemed by Christ, has been called Mystical Rose. She reminds us we are called to the eternal life of Paradise.

A Christian Prayer

Through the centuries, saints like St. Dominic, many of the popes, as well as countless ordinary Christians have found the rosary to be a school of prayer and a source of spiritual blessing. It is both simple and profound. Not beyond anyone's reach, its repeated words bring peace to the soul. And the mysteries of joy, sorrow and glory recalled from Jesus' life are meant to be repeated in our own. Through these mysteries, we hope to "imitate what they contain and obtain what they promise".

From its long experience of this powerful prayer the church today recommends the rosary to all men and women.

Rosary Novenas

A novena is a traditional way of praying in the church. It is nine days of prayers modeled after the nine-day period the apostles prayed before Pentecost. It is a concrete way of praying with perseverance, a quality of prayer Jesus recommended in the gospel.

One type of novena that is popular among some is the "54-day Rosary Novena," which has its origins in 1884 at Naples, Italy, in an apparition of Our Lady of Pompeii. The Novena stipulates that five decades of the rosary are said each day for 27 days in petition, and five decades of the rosary are said each day for the following 27 days in thanksgiving. A table outlining the Joyful, Sorrowful and Glorious Mysteries to be meditated upon over the period is provided on p. 8.

For Petition

1	2	3	4	5	6	7	8	9
J	S	G	J	S	G	J	S	G
10	11	12	13	14	15	16	17	18
J	S	G	J	S	G	J	S	G
19	20	21	22	23	24	25	26	27
J	S	G	J	S	G	J	S	G

In Thanksgiving

1	2	3	4	5	6	7	8	9
J	S	G	J	S	G	J	S	G
10	11	12	13	14	15	16	17	18
J	S	G	J	S	G	J	S	G
19	20	21	22	23	24	25	26	27
J	S	G	J	S	G	J	S	G

HOW TO SAY THE ROSARY

The complete Rosary consists of fifteen decades, but it is further divided into three distinct parts, each containing five decades; the Joyful, the Sorrowful, and the Glorious Mysteries.

To say the Rosary, begin by making the sign of the cross and saying "The Apostles' Creed" on the crucifix, one "Our Father" on the first bead, three "Hail Marys" on the next three beads, and then a "Glory Be to the Father." When this is finished, meditate upon the first mystery, say an "Our Father," ten "Hail Marys," and one "Glory Be to the Father." The first decade is now completed, and to finish the Rosary proceed in the same manner until all five decades have been said.

When this is done, say one "Hail Holy Queen."

PRAYERS OF THE ROSARY

The Sign of the Cross

In the name of the Father, † and of the Son, and of the Holy Spirit. Amen.

The Apostles' Creed

I believe in God, the Father Almighty, Creator of heaven and earth; and in Jesus Christ, His only Son, our Lord, who was conceived by the Holy Spirit; born of the Virgin Mary, suffered under Pontius Pilate, was crucified, died and was buried. He descended into hell; the third day He rose again from the dead; He ascended into heaven, sitteth at the right hand God the Father Almighty; from thence He shall come to judge the living and the dead. I believe in the Holy Spirit, the Holy Catholic Church, the communion of Saints, the forgiveness of sins, the resurrection of the body, and life everlasting. Amen.

The Our Father

Our Father who art in heaven, hallowed be Thy name; Thy kingdom come; Thy will be done on earth as it is in heaven. Give us this day our daily bread; and forgive us our trespasses as we forgive those who trespass against us. And lead us not into temptation; but deliver us from evil. Amen.

The Hail Mary

Hail Mary, full of grace, the Lord is with you;
Blessed are you among women, and blessed is the
fruit of your womb, Jesus. Holy Mary, Mother of
God, pray for us sinners, now and at the hour our
death. Amen.

Glory Be to the Father

Glory be to the Father, and to the Son, and to the
Holy Spirit; as it was in the beginning, is now, and
ever shall be, world without end. Amen.

The Hail, Holy Queen

Hail, holy Queen, Mother of Mercy! Our life, our
sweetness, and our hope! To thee do we cry, poor
banished children of Eve; to thee do we send up
our sighs, mourning and weeping in this valley of
tears. Turn, then, most gracious advocate, thine eyes
of mercy toward us; and after this our exile show
unto us the blessed fruit of thy womb Jesus; O
clement, O loving, O sweet Virgin Mary.

V. Pray for us, O holy Mother of God.
R. That we may be made worthy of the promises of
Christ.

The Five Joyful Mysteries

Mondays and Thursdays
FIRST JOYFUL MYSTERY
> **The Annunciation**
> The Angel Gabriel tells Mary that
> she is to be the Mother of God.

SECOND JOYFUL MYSTERY
> **The Visitation**
> The Blessed Virgin pays a visit to
> her cousin Elizabeth.

THIRD JOYFUL MYSTERY
> **The Birth of Jesus**
> The Infant Jesus is born in a stable
> at Bethlehem.

FOURTH JOYFUL MYSTERY
> **Presentation of Jesus in the Temple**
> The Blessed Virgin presents the Child
> Jesus to Simeon in the Temple.

FIFTH JOYFUL MYSTERY
> **Finding the Child Jesus in the Temple**
> Jesus is lost for three days, and the
> Blessed Mother finds Him in the Temple.

The Joyful Mysteries

Mondays and Thursdays
Sundays of Advent and
after Epiphany until Lent

1st Joyful Mystery
The Annunciation

The Angel Gabriel
appears to Mary,
announcing she is
to be the Mother
of God.
•March 25

5th Joyful Mystery
**The Finding in
the Temple**

The Blessed
Mother finds
Jesus in the
Temple.
•FEAST OF THE
HOLY FAMILY

2nd Joyful Mystery
The Visitation

Elizabeth greets
Mary: "Blessed
art Thou among
women and
blessed is the fruit
of Thy womb!"
•May 31

4th Joyful Mystery
The Presentation

The Blessed Mother
presents the Child
Jesus in the Temple.
•February 2

3rd Joyful Mystery
The Nativity

The Virgin Mary gives
birth to the Redeemer
of the World.
•December 25

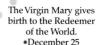

FIRST JOYFUL MYSTERY
The Annunciation
Humility

The Angel Gabriel said: "Do not be afraid, Mary,
you have found favor with God. You will conceive
and bear a Son, and you shall call him Jesus."

LUKE 1, 30-31

Meditation

Nor was Mary afraid to do God's will. The angel left
her, but she was not afraid, even as she faced
Joseph's initial doubt, even though she did not fully
understand it all. She trusted even through the
birth in a poor stable, through the silent years at
Nazareth, the mysterious years of Jesus' ministry
and the darkest hours of His passion and death.

Mary believed God's purpose for her, even though
she did not always understand.

Shall we not say too: "We are your servants, O Lord?"
Shall we not say with Mary, "Be it done to me according
to your word?"

One Our Father, ten Hail Marys and one Glory Be to the
Father.

SECOND JOYFUL MYSTERY
The Visitation *Charity*

Mary visited her cousin, Elizabeth, who said to her,
"Blessed are you among women and blessed is the
fruit of your womb."

LUKE 1, 42

Meditation

Such a simple thing: two cousins visit! One blesses
the other. Mary, with the mighty Child within her,
makes Elizabeth's unborn infant leap for joy. And
the elder Elizabeth speaks words of praise to the
younger Mary. "Blessed are you..."

A simple visit between two people, yet blessings
are exchanged and the two strengthened by God's
grace.

*Help us, O Lord, to make all our meetings with others,
the simple times we share with one another, moments of
joy, faith, love and blessings.*

*One Our Father, ten Hail Marys and one Glory Be to the
Father.*

THIRD JOYFUL MYSTERY
The Birth of Jesus *Poverty*

"Mary gave birth to her first-born son and wrapped him in swaddling clothes and laid him in a manger."

LUKE 2, 7

Meditation

A Child is born for us! In the poorest of places, a stable. With nothing of his own, Jesus Christ was born. He would always be poor, as one of us, and the poor always found a welcome near Him. The shepherds came at the angel's call, leading their sheep. And they returned singing for joy. Later, the blind, the lame and the deaf came. Jesus welcomed them, too. Those possessed by demons, those haunted by fears came; their spirits were lifted and they felt their hearts soar.

Shall we not come too?
"O dying souls, behold your living spring; O dazzled eyes, behold your sun of grace; Dull ears, attend what word this Word doth bring..."

One Our Father, ten Hail Marys and one Glory Be to the Father.

FOURTH JOYFUL MYSTERY
Presentation of Jesus in the Temple

Obedience

"When the time came...they brought the child up to Jerusalem to present him to the Lord."

LUKE 1, 22

Meditation

For Mary and Joseph the time came, shortly after Jesus' birth, to present Him in the temple to God. The time came too for the old man Simeon and the old woman Anna, waiting and praying so long. Waiting in the temple many years, they were hoping God's promises to their people would be fulfilled. The day the tiny Child came, their waiting was rewarded.

"Now dismiss your servant in peace, O Lord, because my eyes have seen your salvation," Simeon said as he took the child in his arms.

May we see what he saw. Give us eyes of faith, O Lord. Renew our hope, reward our waiting, and fill our hearts with joy.

One Our Father, ten Hail Marys and one Glory Be to the Father.

FIFTH JOYFUL MYSTERY
Finding the Child Jesus in the Temple

Piety

"After three days they found Jesus in the Temple, sitting among the teachers and asking them questions."

LUKE 1, 46

Meditation

A special joy comes from finding what we thought lost or seeing what what we were anxious about turn out for the best. The Joyful Mysteries of the Rosary are about such joys: The joys that follow fear, sorrow, struggle and uncertainty.

Look at Mary and Joseph searching for their lost son for three days. Finding Him, their sorrow turns to joy. The lesson is simple: God makes our hearts for joy and will not let us lose treasures that truly matter. Our joy comes from seeking Him.

"Ask and you shall receive,
seek and you shall find,
knock and it shall be opened to you,"
Jesus teaches.

One Our Father, ten Hail Marys, one Glory Be to the Father and one Hail Holy Queen.

The Five Sorrowful Mysteries

Tuesdays and Fridays
FIRST SORROWFUL MYSTERY
> **The Agony in the Garden**
> Jesus prays in the Garden of Olives
> and drops of blood break through
> His skin.

SECOND SORROWFUL MYSTERY
> **The Scourging of Jesus at the Pillar**
> Jesus is tied to a pillar and cruelly
> beaten with whips.

THIRD SORROWFUL MYSTERY
> **Jesus Is Crowned with Thorns**
> A crown of thorns is placed upon
> Jesus' head.

FOURTH SORROWFUL MYSTERY
> **Jesus Carries His Cross**
> Jesus is made to carry His cross
> to Calvary.

FIFTH SORROWFUL MYSTERY
> **The Crucifixion**
> Jesus is nailed to the cross, and
> dies for our sins.

The Sorrowful Mysteries

Tuesdays and Fridays,
Sundays in Lent

1st Sorrowful Mystery
Agony in the Garden

At Gethsemane
Jesus prays as
He contemplates the
sins of the World.
•HOLY THURSDAY

5th Sorrowful Mystery
The Crucifixion

Jesus is nailed to
the cross and
dies after three
hours of Agony.
•GOOD FRIDAY

2nd Sorrowful Mystery
The Scourging

Jesus is cruelly
scourged until His
mortified body could
bear no more.
•CORPUS CHRISTI

4th Sorrowful Mystery
Carrying of the Cross

Jesus carries the heavy
cross upon
His shoulders to Calvary.
•SEPTEMBER 14

3rd Sorrowful Mystery
Crowning with Thorns

A crown of thorns is
placed on the head
of Jesus.
•CHRIST THE KING

FIRST SORROWFUL MYSTERY
The Agony in the Garden *Contrition*

"They went to a place called Gethsemane... and
Jesus became fearful and agitated."

MARK 14, 32

Meditation

Alone on that dark night, among the olive trees in a
garden called Gethsemane, Jesus became fearful
and disturbed. He could have fled, as His disciples
would soon flee. But He stayed, kneeling on the
ground, praying to His Father that the cup of
suffering pass Him by, yet trusting He could drink
it if it be God's will.

As He prayed His spirit grew stronger, and He rose
to face what would come.

*Help us face, O Lord, the darkness where we are tempted
and weak and steady us when we are afraid. By the
mystery of your prayer and agony in the garden, have
mercy on us!*

*One Our Father, ten Hail Marys and one Glory Be to the
Father.*

SECOND SORROWFUL MYSTERY
The Scourging of Jesus at the Pillar

Purity

"Pilate, wishing to please the crowd, released Barabbas, and had Jesus scourged."

MARK 15, 15

Meditation

Seized in the garden, questioned and falsely accused, Jesus was condemned by Pilate, the Roman governor, to be crucified. He was judged a revolutionary, a danger to the people. And the first step for quick Roman justice was scourging: Jesus was lashed with a punishing whip, His body tracked by painful strokes of blood.

"By His stripes we were healed," the Prophet Isaiah said of You, O Lord.

By the wounds of Your scourging, heal us, O Lord.

One Our Father, ten Hail Marys and one Glory Be to the Father.

THIRD SORROWFUL MYSTERY
Jesus Is Crowned with Thorns

Courage

"The soldiers clothed him in a purple cloak and placing a crown of thorns they put it on Him."

MARK 15, 17

Meditation

The Roman soldiers who were to crucify Jesus called their companions to join them in a cruel act of mockery before they led Him to the place of execution. Jesus had claimed to be king; He spoke of a kingdom. Taking His own clothes from Him, the soldiers draped Him in a ragged purple cloak, the color of royalty, and put on His head a crown of sharp thorns. Then they knelt before Him, struck Him, and spat upon Him, saying, "Hail, King of the Jews!"

O Lord Jesus, made a fool and mocked, uphold the dignity of those demeaned by violence and brutality.

One Our Father, ten Hail Marys and one Glory Be to the Father.

FOURTH SORROWFUL MYSTERY
Jesus Carries His Cross   *Patience*

"And He went out bearing His own cross, to the place of the skull, called Golgotha."

JOHN 19, 17

Meditation

From the place of judgment, where He was scourged and mocked, Jesus was led, carrying His cross, outside Jerusalem's walls to Golgotha. Hardly able to walk, He stumbled along the narrow city streets, hurried by the soldiers who wanted a quick execution. Many along the way taunted Him. Most of His friends had deserted Him. Only a few stayed close by His side. Yet, though He seemed at the end of His strength, Jesus kept on.

O Lord Jesus Christ,
you carried your cross.
Be our hope and our strength.

One Our Father, ten Hail Marys and one Glory Be to the Father.

FIFTH SORROWFUL MYSTERY
The Crucifixion
Self-denial

"And they crucified Him, and divided His clothes among them casting lots to decide what each should take."

MARK 15, 24

Meditation

With dreadful skill, the soldiers nailed Jesus to the cross and set it up against the dark sky. "Father, forgive them for they do not know what they are doing," He prayed. He also promised forgiveness to the thief at his side. And seeing His mother, He said to His disciple with her, "Behold, your mother." Though they might kill Him, the love that filled His life would not die. Even the hardened soldiers recognized greatness in this pitiable man. "Truly, He was God's Son!" the centurion exclaimed.

Lord Jesus Christ, who died for us,
give us a love like Yours.

One Our Father, ten Hail Marys, one Glory Be to the Father and one Hail Holy Queen.

The Five Glorious Mysteries

Wednesdays, Saturdays and Sundays
FIRST GLORIOUS MYSTERY
> **The Resurrection of Jesus**
> Jesus rises from the dead, three
> days after His death.

SECOND GLORIOUS MYSTERY
> **The Ascension of Jesus**
> Forty days after His death, Jesus
> ascends into heaven.

THIRD GLORIOUS MYSTERY
> **The Descent of the Holy Spirit**
> Ten days after the Ascension, the
> Holy Spirit comes to the apostles
> and the Blessed Mother in the form
> of fiery tongues.

FOURTH GLORIOUS MYSTERY
> **The Assumption of Mary in Heaven**
> The Blessed Virgin dies and is
> assumed into heaven.

FIFTH GLORIOUS MYSTERY
> **The Crowning of Mary**
> The Blessed Virgin is crowned Queen
> of Heaven and Earth by Jesus, her Son.

The Glorious Mysteries

Wednesdays and
Saturdays
Sundays after Easter
until Advent

1st Glorious Mystery
The Resurrection

Jesus rises glorious
and immortal,
three days after
His death.
•EASTER

5th Glorious Mystery
The Coronation

Mary is gloriously
crowned
Queen of Heaven
and Earth.
•AUGUST 22

2nd Glorious Mystery
The Ascension

Jesus ascends into
Heaven forty days
after His
Resurrection.
•ASCENSION
THURSDAY

4th Glorious Mystery
The Assumption

The Blessed Mother
is united with her
Divine Son in heaven.
•AUGUST 15

3rd Glorious Mystery
Descent of the Holy Spirit

The Holy Spirit
descends upon Mary
and the Apostles.
•PENTECOST

FIRST GLORIOUS MYSTERY
The Resurrection of Jesus

Faith

The angel said: "Do not be afraid...He is not here,
He is risen as He said."

MATTHEW 28, 5-6

Meditation

On Easter Sunday, the women coming to anoint the
body of Jesus were sent away from the tomb, the
place of death. "He is not here," the angel said, "He
is risen."

Then Jesus appeared to His disciples, sometimes to
one and other times to many. Soon even the most
doubtful, like Thomas, were convinced. No, it was
not a ghost or their imagination. They could touch
His wounds with their hands. Jesus was risen from
the dead.

O Lord Jesus Christ, conqueror of death,
help us who believe in You to rise again.

One Our Father, ten Hail Marys and one Glory Be to the
Father.

SECOND GLORIOUS MYSTERY
The Ascension of Jesus

Hope

"As the apostles looked on, Jesus was taken up into heaven out of their sight."

ACTS 1, 9

Meditation

After appearing to His disciples for over forty days, Jesus disappeared from their sight. The gospels see the risen Jesus having a further mission than just returning to life. He has a mission to begin a new creation.

"I go to prepare a place for you," Jesus promises His disciples at the Last Supper. Ascending into heaven, that is what He does: He prepares a place for us, new heavens and a new earth. A home that is ours because of His love for us. It is not only the world of here and now we hope for; we have a home above.

"O Jesus Christ, returned to heaven in victory, remember my flesh in which you were born."

ST. HILARY

One Our Father, ten Hail Marys and one Glory Be to the Father.

THIRD GLORIOUS MYSTERY
The Descent of the Holy Spirit   *Love*

"They were filled with the Holy Spirit and began to speak in tongues as they were given power to speak."

ACTS 2, 2

Meditation

"I will not leave you orphans," Jesus told His disciples. They were to wait for the promised gift of the Father–the gift of the Holy Spirit.

So they waited in Jerusalem until the Jewish feast of Pentecost, fifty days after Easter. Then, as they were all together in one place, a strong wind and sound filled the house, and flames like tongues of fire came to rest on them. They were filled with the Holy Spirit.

The Holy Spirit is Jesus' "first gift to those who believe, to complete His work on earth and bring us the fullness of grace.

"Come, Holy Spirit,
Creator come from Your bright heav'nly throne:
come take possession of our souls,
and make them all Your own."

One Our Father, ten Hail Marys and one Glory Be to the Father.

43

FOURTH GLORIOUS MYSTERY
The Assumption of Mary in Heaven

Eternal Happiness

"We believe that Jesus died and rose again.
Through Jesus, God will bring to life those who
have fallen asleep."

1 THESSALONIANS 4, 14

Meditation

A long tradition supports our belief that Mary, the
mother of Jesus, was assumed body and soul into
heaven. God rewarded her for faithfully fulfilling
her role as the Mother of Jesus. And so, she was
brought to life after falling asleep in death. She was
taken up into heaven.

We see her as a sign of what our future holds. In
the words of the church's liturgy, she brings "hope
and comfort for your people on their pilgrim way."

Pray for us, O holy Mother of God,
that we may be made worthy
of the promises of Christ.

One Our Father, ten Hail Marys and one Glory Be to the
Father.

FIFTH GLORIOUS MYSTERY
The Crowning of Mary   *Devotion to Mary*

"A great sign appeared in the heavens, a woman clothed with the sun, the moon under her feet, and on her head a crown of twelve stars."

REV 12, 1

Meditation

The mysteries of the Rosary begin with a sign the Prophet Isaiah gave: "This is a sign to you: a virgin shall conceive and bear a son, and you will call His name Emmanuel, 'God with us.'" They end urging us to look heavenward, to the sign of a woman clothed in the glories of God's kingdom. Mary, because she stood loyally beside her Son, has become a powerful intercessor at the side of Christ, our heavenly king. She will be a mother to us.

Hail Holy Queen,
mother of mercy,
our life, our sweetness and our hope.
To you we cry,
poor banished children of Eve.

One Our Father, ten Hail Marys, one Glory Be to the
Father and one Hail Holy Queen.

6.
Meditate on
3rd Mystery,
saying the
"Our Father,"
ten "Hail Marys"
and the
"Glory Be."

7.
Meditate on
4th Mystery,
saying the
"Our Father,"
ten "Hail Marys"
and the
"Glory Be."

5.
Meditate on
2nd Mystery,
saying the
"Our Father,"
ten "Hail Marys"
and the
"Glory Be."

8.
Meditate on
5th Mystery,
saying the
"Our Father,"
ten "Hail Mary"
and the
"Glory Be."

4.
Meditate on 1st Mystery,
saying the "Our Father,"
ten "Hail Marys"
and the "Glory Be."

9.
Concluding prayer,
"Hail Holy Queen"

3.
Say three "Hail Marys"
and the "Glory Be."

2.
Say the "Our Father".

1.
Make the Sign of the Cross,
say the Apostles' Creed.